Retirement Planning for Beginners

Simple Strategies to Build Wealth and Secure Your Financial Future

Oliver Lawson

Copyright © 2024 by Oliver Lawson

All rights reserved. No part of this book may be reproduced, distributed, or transmitted in any form or by any means without prior written permission from the author, except for brief quotations in reviews.

Disclaimer

This book provides general information on retirement planning and is not financial advice. Consult a licensed financial advisor for personalized guidance. The author is not liable for any actions taken based on the information provided.

Table of contents

Introduction	7
Chapter 1	11
Understanding Retirement	11
What is Retirement?	11
Why Planning for Retirement is Essential	14
Common Retirement Misconceptions	16
Chapter 2	21
Assessing Your Current Financial Situation	21
Calculating Your Net Worth	21
Evaluating Your Income and Expenses	24
Identifying Your Financial Goals	27
Chapter 3	33
Determining Your Retirement Income Needs	33
Estimating Your Retirement Expenses	33
Considering Inflation and Longevity	37
Factoring in Healthcare and Long-Term Care Costs	41

Chapter 4 — 47
Maximizing Your Retirement Savings — 47

Employer-Sponsored Retirement Plans (401(k), 403(b), etc.) — 47

Individual Retirement Accounts (IRAs) — 52

Other Savings Vehicles (HSAs, Taxable Accounts) — 55

Chapter 5 — 61
Investing for Retirement — 61

Understanding Asset Allocation — 61

Choosing the Right Investment Mix — 66

Rebalancing Your Portfolio — 71

Chapter 6 — 77
Retirement Income Distribution Strategies — 77

Sustainable Withdrawal Rates — 77

Sequence of Returns Risk and Mitigation Strategies — 82

Annuities and Other Income-Generating Options — 87

Chapter 7 — 93
Exploring Additional Income Sources — 93

Social Security Benefits Optimization ... 93

Pension Plans and Lump-Sum Options ... 98

Reverse Mortgages and Home Equity ... 103

Chapter 8 — 109

Minimizing Taxes in Retirement — 109

Tax-Efficient Withdrawal Strategies ... 109

Roth Conversions and Tax Diversification ... 114

Charitable Giving and Estate Planning ... 119

Chapter 9 — 125

Creating a Comprehensive Retirement Plan — 125

Putting the Pieces Together ... 125

Stress-Testing Your Plan and Preparing for the Unexpected ... 130

The Importance of Working with Financial Professionals ... 135

Chapter 10 — 141

Enjoying Your Retirement — 141

Retirement Lifestyle Planning (Housing, Travel, Budgeting) ... 141

Maintaining Physical and Mental Health in Retirement 146

Finding Purpose, Fulfillment, and Leaving a Legacy 152

Introduction

You're standing at the edge of a vast, unexplored wilderness. Before you lies a winding path, full of potential and possibility, but also shrouded in uncertainty. This path is your retirement journey, and like any great adventure, it requires careful planning and preparation to navigate successfully.

For many of us, retirement feels like a distant dream, something we'll worry about later when we have more time, more money, or more gray hair. But the truth is, the earlier you start planning for retirement, the better equipped you'll be to make that dream a reality.

Think of retirement planning like packing for a long hiking trip. You wouldn't wait until the morning of the hike to start throwing things into your backpack haphazardly. Instead, you'd take time to carefully consider what you need: sturdy shoes, warm layers, plenty of food and water, a map to guide your way. The same principle applies to your retirement. The sooner you start "packing your bag" with smart financial decisions and strategic plans, the more prepared you'll be for the journey ahead.

But where do you begin? The world of retirement planning can feel overwhelming, full of complex terms, confusing options, and conflicting advice. It's easy to become paralyzed by the choices or to put off making decisions because you don't feel like you know enough.

That's where this book comes in. Consider it your trusty guide on the retirement planning trail - a comprehensive, step-by-step roadmap to help you navigate the wilderness of saving, investing, and preparing for your post-career life.

In the pages ahead, we'll demystify the jargon, break down the concepts, and provide practical, actionable advice that you can start implementing today, no matter your age, income, or financial background. We'll cover everything from understanding your retirement needs and maximizing your savings to creating an investment strategy, managing risks, and even planning for the more nuanced aspects of retirement, like healthcare, estate planning, and finding a sense of purpose and fulfillment.

The journey to retirement is different for everyone, full of unique challenges, priorities, and aspirations. There's no one-size-fits-all approach to planning for this major life transition. That's why this book is designed to meet you where you are, whether you're just starting your first job or nearing the end of your career. We'll provide a range of strategies and scenarios that you can adapt to your specific situation, as well as interactive exercises and resources to help you put the principles into practice.

But this book isn't just about the nuts and bolts of retirement planning. It's also about empowering you to take control of your financial future, to make informed choices that align with your values and goals, and to approach retirement not with fear or uncertainty, but with confidence and optimism.

Because here's the truth: Retirement planning isn't just about money. It's about crafting a vision for the life you want to lead after your working years are over. It's about having the freedom and resources to pursue your passions, to spend time with the people you love, to make a difference in your community and the world around you. It's about writing the next great chapter in your life story.

No matter where you are on the path to retirement, it's never too early (or too late) to start planning. By picking up this book, you've already taken the first step on a journey that will shape the course of your future. So let's dive in, together, and start mapping out the retirement of your dreams. The wilderness awaits, and with the right tools, knowledge, and mindset, you'll be ready to blaze your own trail to a fulfilling and financially secure post-career life.

Chapter 1

Understanding Retirement

What is Retirement?

Retirement is a significant milestone in one's life, marking the end of a career and the beginning of a new chapter. It is a time when an individual transitions from the workforce to a life of leisure, personal pursuits, and, for some, a chance to redefine their purpose. Traditionally, retirement was associated with reaching a specific age, such as 65, and was often accompanied by a gold watch and a farewell party. However, the concept of retirement has evolved over time, and today, it means different things to different people.

For some, retirement is a complete cessation of work, a time to enjoy the fruits of their labor and pursue hobbies and interests that were previously limited by the demands of a full-time job. This may include traveling, spending more time with family and friends, volunteering, or taking up new hobbies like gardening, painting, or learning a musical instrument.

Others view retirement as a shift in their work life, transitioning from a full-time career to part-time work or entrepreneurship. This approach allows individuals to maintain a sense of purpose and continue earning an income while enjoying more flexibility and freedom in their schedules.

Another perspective on retirement is the achievement of financial independence, where an individual has accumulated sufficient assets and passive income streams to cover their living expenses without the need for traditional employment. This concept, often referred to as "FIRE" (Financial Independence, Retire Early), has gained popularity in recent years, with many people striving to save aggressively and invest wisely to retire earlier than the conventional age.

Regardless of how one defines retirement, it is a time of significant change and adjustment. Retirees must adapt to a new routine, find ways to stay socially connected, and maintain a sense of purpose and fulfillment. They must also navigate the financial challenges of living on a fixed income and ensuring that their savings last throughout their retirement years.

In essence, retirement is a unique and personal journey that marks the end of one chapter and the beginning of another. It is an opportunity to redefine oneself, pursue new passions, and enjoy the rewards of a lifetime of hard work. As such, it is crucial to approach retirement with careful planning and consideration to ensure a smooth transition and a fulfilling post-work life.

Why Planning for Retirement is Essential

Planning for retirement is one of the most important financial decisions an individual can make. It is a process that involves setting goals, assessing one's current financial situation, and developing a roadmap to achieve a secure and comfortable retirement. Without proper planning, individuals may face financial challenges and uncertainty in their golden years.

One of the primary reasons retirement planning is essential is the fact that people are living longer. Advances in healthcare and technology have increased life expectancy, meaning that retirees may spend 20, 30, or even 40 years in retirement. This longevity requires a significant amount of savings to ensure that one's financial resources last throughout their retirement years.

Another factor that underscores the importance of retirement planning is the shift away from traditional pension plans. In the past, many employers offered defined benefit pension plans that guaranteed a steady stream of income in retirement. However, these plans have become increasingly rare, with most employers now offering defined contribution plans, such as 401(k)s, which place the responsibility of saving and investing for retirement on the individual.

Moreover, retirement planning is crucial because of the rising cost of healthcare. As individuals age, they are more likely to experience health issues that require medical attention and treatment. In the United States, healthcare costs have been increasing at a rate that outpaces inflation, making it essential for retirees to have sufficient savings to cover these expenses.

Retirement planning also helps individuals to determine their retirement income needs and develop a strategy to meet those needs. This process involves estimating one's expenses in retirement, factoring in inflation, and creating a budget that aligns with their desired lifestyle. By planning ahead, individuals can make informed decisions about their savings and investments, ensuring that they have a diversified portfolio that can withstand market volatility and provide a steady stream of income in retirement.

Furthermore, retirement planning allows individuals to take advantage of tax-efficient savings vehicles, such as 401(k)s and IRAs. These accounts offer tax benefits that can help individuals to save more for retirement while minimizing their tax liability. By starting to save early and consistently, individuals can harness the power of compound interest to grow their retirement nest egg over time.

Common Retirement Misconceptions

As individuals navigate the complex landscape of retirement planning, they may encounter several misconceptions that can lead to poor decision-making and financial setbacks. These misconceptions can be rooted in outdated information, misinterpretation of data, or simply a lack of understanding about the realities of retirement. By addressing and dispelling these common misconceptions, individuals can approach retirement planning with a clearer and more accurate perspective.

One of the most pervasive retirement misconceptions is the belief that Social Security will provide sufficient income to cover all of one's expenses in retirement. While Social Security is an important source of retirement income for many Americans, it was never intended to be the sole source of income. On average, Social Security benefits replace only about 40% of pre-retirement income, leaving a significant gap that must be filled by personal savings and investments.

Another common misconception is that one's expenses will decrease significantly in retirement. While some expenses, such as commuting costs and work-related expenses, may indeed decrease, others, such as healthcare costs and leisure activities, may increase.

Additionally, retirees must account for the impact of inflation, which can erode the purchasing power of their savings over time. As a result, it is crucial for individuals to create a realistic budget that accounts for their anticipated expenses in retirement.

Many people also believe that they can postpone saving for retirement until later in their careers when they are earning more money. However, this approach fails to recognize the power of compound interest and the importance of starting to save early. By starting to save in one's 20s or 30s, individuals can benefit from decades of compounding growth, making it easier to accumulate a significant retirement nest egg. Conversely, those who wait until later in their careers to start saving may find it challenging to catch up and may need to save a larger portion of their income to reach their retirement goals.

Another misconception is that one's investment portfolio should become more conservative as they approach retirement. While it is true that individuals may want to reduce their exposure to risk as they near retirement, shifting to an overly conservative portfolio can be counterproductive. With longer life expectancies, retirees may need to maintain some exposure to growth-oriented investments to ensure that their savings last throughout their retirement years. A well-diversified portfolio that balances risk and return can help retirees to meet their long-term financial goals.

Finally, some individuals believe that they can rely on their children or other family members for financial support in retirement. However, this assumption can place an undue burden on family members and may not be a reliable or sustainable solution. It is essential for individuals to take responsibility for their own retirement planning and to develop a plan that ensures their financial independence and security.

In conclusion, retirement planning is a complex process that requires a clear understanding of one's financial situation, goals, and the realities of retirement. By dispelling common misconceptions and seeking accurate information and guidance, individuals can make informed decisions that will help them to achieve a secure and fulfilling retirement. Whether it is starting to save early, creating a realistic budget, or maintaining a well-diversified investment portfolio, taking a proactive and informed approach to retirement planning is essential for long-term financial success.

Chapter 2

Assessing Your Current Financial Situation

Calculating Your Net Worth

The first step in assessing your current financial situation is to calculate your net worth. Your net worth is the total value of all your assets minus the total value of all your liabilities. Think of it like a snapshot that captures your financial health at a specific point in time.

Let's break this down. Your assets include everything you own that has monetary value. This could be your house, your car, your savings and investment accounts, valuable jewelry or art, and even the cash in your wallet. Imagine gathering up all these items and adding price tags to each of them. The sum of all those price tags is the total value of your assets.

On the other side of the equation are your liabilities. These are all the debts and financial obligations you owe to others. Common liabilities include your mortgage, car loans, student loans, credit card balances, and any other bills or debts you haven't paid off yet. Picture all these debts as weights pulling down on your financial standing.

To calculate your net worth, you simply take the total value of your assets and subtract the total value of your liabilities. If your assets are worth more than your debts, you have a positive net worth. This is a good sign, as it means you own more than you owe. On the other hand, if your liabilities outweigh your assets, your net worth is negative. This indicates that you owe more money than the value of what you own.

Here's a simple example to illustrate the concept: Let's say John owns a house worth $200,000, a car worth

$15,000, and has $10,000 in his savings account. His total assets are $225,000. However, John also has a mortgage balance of $150,000, a car loan of $10,000, and credit card debt of $5,000. His total liabilities are $165,000. To find his net worth, John subtracts his liabilities from his assets: $225,000 - $165,000 = $60,000. John's net worth is $60,000.

Calculating your net worth is important because it gives you a clear picture of your financial starting point. It's like a baseline measurement that you can use to track your financial progress over time. By regularly updating your net worth calculation, you can see how your financial decisions and life events impact your overall financial health.

If your net worth is negative or lower than you'd like, don't be discouraged. This knowledge empowers you to make changes and take control of your financial future. You might decide to focus on paying down debt, increasing your income, or investing more money to grow your assets. On the other hand, if your net worth is positive and growing, you can feel confident that you're on the right track and make plans to maintain and enhance your financial well-being.

Evaluating Your Income and Expenses

Once you have a clear picture of your overall financial standing from calculating your net worth, the next step is to dive deeper into the flow of money in your life. This means taking a close look at your income and expenses.

Your income is all the money that comes into your household from various sources. This typically includes your salary from your job, but it can also encompass freelance earnings, investment returns, rental income, government benefits, and any other regular or occasional influxes of money. Think of your income as the river that feeds your financial landscape.

To get a handle on your income, it's helpful to look at your pay stubs, bank statements, and any other records of money coming in. Don't forget to account for any deductions, such as taxes or retirement contributions, to arrive at your take-home pay. If your income varies from month to month, it's a good idea to calculate an average over a longer period, like six months or a year, to get a more accurate sense of your typical earnings.

On the other side of the cash flow equation are your expenses. These are all the ways money flows out of your life, like water draining through holes in a bucket. Expenses include everything you spend money on, from necessities like housing, food, and transportation to discretionary purchases like entertainment, dining out, and travel.

To understand your expenses, you'll need to track your spending. You can do this by combing through your bank and credit card statements, keeping a spending diary, or using a budgeting app. As you review your expenses, it's helpful to categorize them. Common expense categories include housing, utilities, food, transportation, health care, insurance, debt payments, savings, and personal spending.

Once you have a comprehensive list of your expenses, you can total them up and compare the sum to your income. If your income exceeds your expenses, you have a surplus. This extra money can be used to save for future goals, pay off debt faster, or invest for growth. On the other hand, if your expenses outstrip your income, you have a deficit. This means you're spending more money than you're bringing in, which can lead to debt and financial stress if not addressed.

Evaluating your income and expenses is like giving your financial life a check-up. It helps you see where your money is coming from and where it's going. This awareness is crucial for making informed financial decisions and setting realistic goals.

If you discover that you're spending more than you'd like in certain areas, you can look for ways to cut back or find more affordable alternatives. If you find that your income is barely covering your expenses, you might decide to look for ways to increase your earnings, such as asking for a raise, finding a higher-paying job, or starting a side hustle.

Remember, the goal is not to judge yourself harshly, but rather to empower yourself with knowledge. By understanding your income and expenses, you can make deliberate choices about how to allocate your money in a way that aligns with your values and goals. This is a key step in taking control of your financial life and building a strong foundation for your future.

Identifying Your Financial Goals

With a clear understanding of your net worth and cash flow, you're ready to start thinking about your financial future. This is where setting financial goals comes in. Your financial goals are the destinations you want your money to take you to. They're the things you want to achieve or acquire through the power of your financial resources.

Financial goals can be short-term, like saving for a vacation or a down payment on a car, or long-term, like saving for retirement or your children's education. They can also be categorized as needs, wants, or wishes. Needs are essential expenses, like housing and food. Wants are things that improve your quality of life but aren't strictly necessary, like a new smartphone or a gym membership. Wishes are aspirational desires, like owning a vacation home or traveling the world.

To identify your financial goals, start by dreaming big. Imagine your ideal financial future. What does it look like? Do you want to be debt-free? Own your own home? Have a comfortable retirement? Be able to afford big experiences like world travel? Write down all your aspirations, no matter how grand or small.

Next, prioritize your goals. Which ones are most important to you? Which ones do you want to achieve first? Consider factors like your values, your life stage, and your family situation. For example, if you have young children, saving for their education might be a top priority. If you're nearing retirement age, ensuring you have enough savings to support your desired lifestyle might be your primary focus.

Once you have your prioritized list of goals, make them SMART. SMART is an acronym that stands for Specific, Measurable, Achievable, Relevant, and Time-bound. A SMART goal is clear and well-defined, with a specific outcome and deadline. For example, instead of "save for retirement," a SMART goal might be "save $500,000 in my retirement accounts by age 65." This goal specifies an amount, a location, and a time frame, making it easier to plan for and track progress.

For each of your SMART goals, estimate how much money you'll need to achieve them. This might involve some research, like looking up the cost of tuition at your child's dream college or the average price of homes in your desired neighborhood. Don't get too bogged down in the details; ballpark estimates are fine for now. The idea is to get a general sense of the financial targets you're aiming for.

Finally, consider the time horizon for each goal. When do you want to achieve it by? This will help you determine how much you need to save or invest each month or year to stay on track. For long-term goals, you'll also need to consider factors like inflation and potential investment returns, which can impact how much you'll ultimately need to save.

Identifying your financial goals is a crucial step in creating a roadmap for your financial future. By clarifying what you want to achieve with your money, you can make intentional choices about how to allocate your income and prioritize your spending. Your goals will guide your financial decisions and motivate you to stay disciplined with your saving and investing habits.

Remember, your goals are not set in stone. Life circumstances change, priorities shift, and new dreams emerge. Regularly review and adjust your goals as needed to ensure they still align with your values and desires. The key is to keep your eyes on the prize while remaining flexible and adaptable along the way.

Chapter 3

Determining Your Retirement Needs Income

Estimating Your Retirement Expenses

One of the most crucial aspects of retirement planning is estimating your expenses during your golden years. This step is essential because it forms the foundation for determining how much income you'll need to maintain your desired lifestyle in retirement. Without a clear understanding of your anticipated expenses, it's challenging to set realistic savings goals or make informed decisions about your retirement income strategies.

To begin estimating your retirement expenses, start by examining your current spending habits. Review your bank statements, credit card bills, and receipts to get a sense of where your money is going each month. Categorize your expenses into essential and discretionary items. Essential expenses include things like housing, food, utilities, transportation, and healthcare, while discretionary expenses encompass entertainment, travel, hobbies, and other non-essential purchases.

Next, consider how your expenses might change in retirement. Some costs, such as commuting and work-related expenses, may decrease or disappear entirely. However, other expenses, like travel and leisure activities, may increase as you have more time to pursue your interests. Additionally, it's essential to factor in the potential for new expenses, such as healthcare costs, which we'll discuss in more detail later.

One helpful approach to estimating your retirement expenses is to create a hypothetical retirement budget.

Start with your current monthly expenses and adjust them based on how you expect your lifestyle to change in retirement. For example, if you plan to downsize your home or relocate to a more affordable area, your housing costs may decrease. Conversely, if you anticipate traveling more frequently, your travel and leisure expenses may increase.

When creating your retirement budget, be sure to account for both fixed and variable expenses. Fixed expenses, such as housing costs and insurance premiums, remain relatively stable from month to month. Variable expenses, like groceries and entertainment, can fluctuate based on your lifestyle and choices. It's essential to build some flexibility into your budget to accommodate these fluctuations and unexpected expenses.

Another factor to consider when estimating your retirement expenses is your desired retirement lifestyle. Do you envision a modest, simple retirement, or do you dream of a more luxurious lifestyle filled with travel and adventure? Your retirement lifestyle will significantly impact your expenses and, consequently, the amount of income you'll need to support it.

One way to gauge your retirement lifestyle is to consider your current standard of living. If you're satisfied with your current lifestyle and expect to maintain a similar standard of living in retirement, you can use your current expenses as a baseline for your retirement budget. However, if you anticipate significant changes, such as increased travel or pursuing expensive hobbies, you'll need to adjust your budget accordingly.

It's also important to remember that your retirement expenses may not remain constant throughout your retirement years. In the early stages of retirement, you may be more active and incur higher expenses related to travel, leisure activities, and hobbies. As you age, your expenses may shift towards healthcare and long-term care costs. Consider creating separate budgets for different phases of retirement to account for these changes.

Estimating your retirement expenses is not an exact science, and it's essential to build some wiggle room into your budget to accommodate unexpected costs and changes in your lifestyle. A good rule of thumb is to plan for expenses that are 70-80% of your pre-retirement income, but this can vary depending on your unique circumstances and goals.

Considering Inflation and Longevity

When planning for retirement, it's crucial to consider two critical factors that can significantly impact your financial well-being: inflation and longevity. Failing to account for these factors can lead to underestimating your retirement income needs and potentially running out of money in your later years. Let's explore each of these factors in more detail.

Inflation is the gradual increase in the price of goods and services over time, which erodes the purchasing power of your money. In other words, as inflation rises, each dollar you have buys less than it did in the past. For example, if the cost of a gallon of milk is $3 today and the annual inflation rate is 2%, that same gallon of milk would cost $3.06 next year.

While a 2% inflation rate may not seem significant on a year-to-year basis, its cumulative effect over a long retirement can be substantial. Consider this: if you retire at age 65 and live to age 90 (a 25-year retirement), with an annual inflation rate of 2%, your expenses would nearly double during that time. In other words, if you need $50,000 per year to cover your expenses at the start of retirement, you would need almost $100,000 per year by the end of retirement to maintain the same standard of living.

To account for inflation in your retirement planning, you'll need to factor it into your estimated retirement expenses. One approach is to use a retirement calculator that includes an inflation adjustment. These calculators typically allow you to input an assumed annual inflation rate (e.g., 2% or 3%) and will adjust your projected expenses accordingly.

Another strategy is to invest a portion of your retirement savings in assets that have the potential to outpace inflation, such as stocks and real estate. While these investments come with some risk, they have historically provided returns that exceed the rate of inflation over the long term.

Longevity is another critical factor to consider when planning for retirement. Thanks to advances in healthcare and technology, people are living longer than ever before. According to the Social Security Administration, a 65-year-old man today can expect to live, on average, until age 84, while a 65-year-old woman can expect to live until age 86.5. However, these are just averages, and many people will live well beyond these ages.

The challenge with longevity is that the longer you live, the more years you'll need to fund in retirement. If you underestimate your life expectancy and plan for a shorter retirement, you risk outliving your savings and struggling financially in your later years. On the other hand, if you overestimate your life expectancy and save too much, you may unnecessarily sacrifice your quality of life during your working years.

To account for longevity in your retirement planning, consider using a life expectancy calculator to get a sense of how long you might live based on your age, gender, and health factors. Keep in mind, however, that these calculators provide estimates, and there's no guarantee that you'll live to a specific age.

One strategy to hedge against longevity risk is to plan for a longer retirement than you expect. For example, if you estimate that you'll live to age 90, consider planning for a retirement that lasts until age 95 or even 100. This extra cushion can provide peace of mind and ensure that you don't run out of money in your later years.

Another approach is to consider products like annuities, which can provide a guaranteed stream of income for life, regardless of how long you live. While annuities can be complex and may not be appropriate for everyone, they can be a useful tool for managing longevity risk.

Factoring in Healthcare and Long-Term Care Costs

When planning for retirement, it's easy to focus on the fun aspects, like travel and leisure activities. However, it's crucial not to overlook two significant expenses that can have a major impact on your retirement budget: healthcare and long-term care costs. These expenses are often unpredictable and can quickly derail your retirement plans if you're not prepared for them. Let's take a closer look at each of these costs and how to factor them into your retirement income needs.

Healthcare costs are a significant concern for retirees, and for good reason. According to the Fidelity Retiree Health Care Cost Estimate, the average 65-year-old couple retiring in 2021 can expect to spend approximately $300,000 on healthcare expenses throughout their retirement, not including long-term care costs. This estimate includes premiums, deductibles, copayments, and out-of-pocket expenses for medical, dental, and vision care.

Several factors contribute to the high cost of healthcare in retirement. First, as we age, we're more likely to develop chronic health conditions that require ongoing medical treatment. Second, the cost of healthcare services and prescription drugs continues to rise faster than the general inflation rate. Finally, while Medicare provides health insurance coverage for retirees, it doesn't cover everything, and there are still significant out-of-pocket costs.

To factor healthcare costs into your retirement income needs, start by understanding what Medicare does and doesn't cover. Medicare Part A (hospital insurance) and Part B (medical insurance) cover a portion of your healthcare expenses, but there are deductibles, copayments, and coinsurance amounts that you'll be responsible for paying out of pocket. Additionally, Medicare doesn't cover most dental, vision, or hearing care, nor does it cover long-term care expenses.

One option to help cover the gaps in Medicare coverage is to purchase a Medicare Supplement Insurance (Medigap) policy. These policies are offered by private insurance companies and can help pay for some of the out-of-pocket costs associated with Medicare, such as deductibles and copayments. Another option is to enroll in a Medicare Advantage Plan (Part C), which combines Part A and B coverage with additional benefits like dental and vision care.

To estimate your healthcare costs in retirement, consider using a healthcare cost calculator. These tools can help you project your potential expenses based on your age, health status, and coverage options. Keep in mind that these are just estimates, and your actual costs may vary depending on your individual circumstances.

In addition to healthcare costs, it's essential to consider the potential for long-term care expenses in retirement. Long-term care refers to the assistance and support needed when someone can no longer perform activities of daily living, such as bathing, dressing, and eating, due to a chronic illness, disability, or cognitive impairment like Alzheimer's disease.

The cost of long-term care services can be staggering. According to the Genworth Cost of Care Survey, the median annual cost for a private room in a nursing home in 2020 was over $100,000, while the median annual cost for home health aide services was over $50,000. These costs vary widely by location and can quickly deplete your retirement savings if you're not prepared.

To factor long-term care costs into your retirement income needs, consider the likelihood that you'll need these services and for how long. While it's impossible to predict with certainty, factors like your family health history, lifestyle, and personal preferences can provide some guidance.

One option to help cover the cost of long-term care is to purchase long-term care insurance. These policies can help pay for the cost of care in a variety of settings, including nursing homes, assisted living facilities, and your own home. However, these policies can be expensive, and not everyone will qualify depending on their age and health status.

Another option is to plan to self-fund your long-term care expenses using your retirement savings and assets. This approach requires significant savings and careful planning to ensure that you have enough money to cover both your long-term care needs and your other retirement expenses.

Chapter 4

Maximizing Your Retirement Savings

Employer-Sponsored Retirement Plans (401(k), 403(b), etc.)

Imagine you're setting out on a long hike up a mountain. Your goal is to reach the summit, which represents a comfortable retirement. One of the most effective tools you have to help you climb that mountain is an employer-sponsored retirement plan, such as a 401(k) or 403(b).

Think of these plans as a powerful set of hiking poles that can give you extra stability and momentum on your journey. When you participate in a 401(k) or similar plan, you're essentially giving yourself a boost with each paycheck, setting aside a portion of your earnings to propel you towards your retirement goals.

The real magic of these plans lies in a concept called pre-tax contributions. When you contribute to a traditional 401(k), the money goes into your account before taxes are taken out. It's like having a secret passageway that allows you to bypass the tax tollbooth on your way to saving for retirement. This means you can lower your current taxable income and potentially pay less in taxes each year, all while building your retirement nest egg.

But the benefits don't stop there. Many employers offer something called a matching contribution. This is essentially free money that your employer adds to your retirement account based on how much you contribute. For example, your employer might match 50% of your contributions up to a certain percentage of your salary. So if you contribute 6% of your salary and your employer matches half of that, you're effectively getting a 3% raise in the form of retirement savings. It's like having a trail guide who's willing to carry some of your gear for you, lightening your load as you climb towards retirement.

Another advantage of employer-sponsored plans is that they make saving automatic and painless. Once you set up your contributions, the money is automatically deducted from your paycheck and deposited into your retirement account. You don't have to remember to transfer money each month or make a conscious decision to save. It's like having a GPS device that automatically keeps you on the right trail, even when the path gets rocky or you're feeling tired.

Over time, these automatic contributions can really add up thanks to the power of compound growth. When you invest your money, you earn returns not only on your initial investment but also on your accumulated earnings. It's like a snowball rolling down a hill, getting bigger and bigger as it goes. The earlier you start saving in your career, the more time your money has to grow and compound.

Of course, like any hike, there may be some uphill battles along the way. The stock market, where most 401(k) funds are invested, can be volatile in the short term, with plenty of ups and downs. But historically, over the long term, the stock market has trended upwards. By consistently contributing to your 401(k) over the course of your career, you can help smooth out those short-term bumps and benefit from long-term growth.

So how do you make the most of your employer-sponsored plan? First, try to contribute as much as you can, or at least enough to earn the full employer match. That match is essentially a guaranteed return on your investment, so it's wise to take full advantage of it. Second, pay attention to the investment options available in your plan and choose a diversified mix of funds that aligns with your risk tolerance and retirement timeline. Many plans offer target-date funds that automatically adjust your investment mix as you near retirement, which can be a simple way to stay on track.

Finally, resist the temptation to tap into your 401(k) before retirement unless absolutely necessary. Withdrawing money early can incur steep penalties and taxes, not to mention sabotaging your long-term savings. Your 401(k) is designed to be a long-term investment vehicle to support you in retirement, not a rainy-day fund for short-term expenses.

In essence, maximizing your employer-sponsored retirement plan is one of the most powerful steps you can take on your journey to a secure retirement. By taking advantage of pre-tax contributions, employer matching, automatic savings, and the power of compound growth, you'll be well on your way to reaching that mountaintop view of a comfortable retirement.

Individual Retirement Accounts (IRAs)

Continuing with our hiking analogy, think of Individual Retirement Accounts (IRAs) as a complementary set of tools to your employer-sponsored plans, like a sturdy pair of hiking boots. While your 401(k) or 403(b) forms the backbone of your retirement savings strategy, IRAs can provide additional support and flexibility on your journey to retirement.

There are two main types of IRAs: traditional and Roth. Each offers unique benefits and operates a bit differently, just like different types of hiking boots are suited for different terrains and weather conditions.

Traditional IRA contributions are tax-deductible, meaning they can lower your taxable income for the year, similar to traditional 401(k) contributions. The money you contribute can then grow tax-deferred over time. It's like taking a detour on your hike that allows you to bypass some rocky, tax-heavy terrain. However, when you withdraw money from a traditional IRA in retirement, those withdrawals are taxed as ordinary income, just as if you were receiving a paycheck. Think of it as reaching a peaceful valley in retirement, but having to pay a toll to enter and enjoy the scenery.

On the other hand, Roth IRA contributions are made with after-tax dollars, meaning there's no immediate tax benefit. However, the real advantage comes later: your money can grow tax-free, and you can generally make tax-free withdrawals in retirement. It's like hiking through some rugged, tax-heavy terrain upfront, but being rewarded with a serene, tax-free lake at the end of your journey.

So how do you decide between a traditional and Roth IRA? It primarily depends on your current tax situation and your expectations for the future. If you think you're in a higher tax bracket now than you will be in retirement, a traditional IRA may make sense, as you can get a tax break now when it's most beneficial. But if you're in a lower tax bracket now and expect to be in a higher one in retirement, a Roth IRA may be the better choice, as you'll pay taxes now at a lower rate and enjoy tax-free withdrawals later.

One key difference between IRAs and 401(k)s is that IRAs are not employer-sponsored. You open an IRA on your own with a financial institution of your choice. This means you have more control and a wider variety of investment options, but it also means you're responsible for making your own contributions and investment decisions. It's like being a solo hiker responsible for navigating your own trail, rather than following a pre-planned route with a guide.

Another important factor to consider is the contribution limits. As of 2023, you can contribute up to $6,500 per year to an IRA ($7,500 if you're 50 or older). This is lower than the contribution limit for 401(k)s, which is $22,500 ($30,000 if you're 50 or older). However, if you don't have access to an employer-sponsored plan, or if you've already maxed out your 401(k) contributions, an IRA can be a valuable additional savings tool.

Like 401(k)s, IRAs are designed to be long-term savings vehicles for retirement. Withdrawing money before age 59½ generally incurs a 10% early withdrawal penalty, in addition to any taxes owed. However, there are some exceptions, such as using the money for qualified first-time home purchases, certain educational expenses, or if you become disabled.

Other Savings Vehicles (HSAs, Taxable Accounts)

While employer-sponsored plans like 401(k)s and individual retirement accounts (IRAs) form the core of most people's retirement savings strategy, there are other savings vehicles that can provide additional support and flexibility on your journey to retirement. Think of these as supplementary tools in your hiking kit, like a hydration pack or trekking poles, that can make your hike more comfortable and efficient.

One such tool is a Health Savings Account (HSA). HSAs are designed to help individuals with high-deductible health plans (HDHPs) save for medical expenses, but they can also serve as a powerful retirement savings vehicle. Contributions to HSAs are tax-deductible, the money grows tax-free, and withdrawals are tax-free if used for qualified medical expenses. It's like having a secret oasis along your hiking trail where you can refill your water without having to pay for it.

The real power of HSAs lies in their triple tax advantage. Not only do you get a tax deduction for your contributions, but your money also grows tax-free, and you can make tax-free withdrawals for qualified medical expenses. In retirement, you can use your HSA funds to pay for Medicare premiums, long-term care insurance, and other healthcare costs. And once you turn 65, you can use your HSA money for any purpose without penalty, though you'll have to pay ordinary income taxes on non-medical withdrawals, similar to a traditional IRA.

To contribute to an HSA, you must be enrolled in an HDHP. In 2023, you can contribute up to $3,850 for individual coverage or $7,750 for family coverage, with an additional $1,000 catch-up contribution allowed if you're 55 or older. If you have the means to max out your other retirement accounts, contributing to an HSA can provide an additional tax-advantaged savings boost, especially if you anticipate significant healthcare costs in retirement.

Another savings tool to consider is a taxable investment account. While taxable accounts don't offer the same tax advantages as 401(k)s, IRAs, or HSAs, they can still play a valuable role in your retirement savings plan. Think of them as a versatile multi-tool that can help you tackle a variety of financial challenges on your hike.

The main advantage of taxable accounts is their flexibility. Unlike retirement accounts, there are no contribution limits, income restrictions, or withdrawal penalties. You can invest as much as you want, in a wide variety of assets, and access your money at any time without incurring early withdrawal fees. This makes taxable accounts a good option for savings goals outside of retirement, such as saving for a down payment on a house or funding a child's education.

However, the trade-off for this flexibility is that you don't get the same tax breaks as you do with retirement accounts. You'll have to pay taxes on your investment earnings, such as dividends and capital gains, in the year they're realized. Long-term capital gains (for assets held longer than a year) are taxed at a lower rate than ordinary income, but it's still a consideration.

Despite the tax implications, taxable accounts can still be a smart addition to your retirement savings plan. They can provide a source of funds in early retirement, before you're able to access your 401(k) or IRA without penalty. They can also help you diversify your tax exposure in retirement, as you'll have a mix of taxable, tax-deferred, and potentially tax-free (in the case of Roth accounts) income sources to draw from.

When investing in a taxable account, it's important to be mindful of tax efficiency. This means choosing investments that minimize taxable events, such as low-turnover index funds or municipal bonds (which are exempt from federal and sometimes state taxes). It also means being strategic about when you sell investments, as you can offset capital gains with capital losses to reduce your tax bill.

In the grand scheme of your retirement journey, taxable accounts are like a side trail that can offer some scenic views and alternate routes to your destination. While they may not be the main path, they can provide valuable support and flexibility as you navigate the financial wilderness.

Whether you're using an HSA to save for healthcare costs, a taxable account to supplement your retirement income, or a combination of various savings vehicles, the key is to stay focused on your ultimate goal: a secure and comfortable retirement. By understanding the features and benefits of each tool at your disposal, you can create a comprehensive savings plan that helps you overcome obstacles, weather the ups and downs of the market, and reach your retirement summit with confidence.

Chapter 5

Investing for Retirement

Understanding Asset Allocation

Asset allocation is one of the most crucial decisions you'll make when investing for retirement. It refers to how you divide your investment portfolio among different asset classes, such as stocks, bonds, and cash. Think of it as deciding what supplies to pack for a long hiking trip – you'll want a balanced mix of items to keep you safe, comfortable and well-nourished in various trail conditions.

Just as you wouldn't pack only sunscreen or only rain gear for a hike, you don't want to put all your money in one type of investment. Each asset class has its own unique characteristics and responds differently to economic conditions. By spreading your money across different asset classes, you can potentially balance risk and reward in your portfolio.

Let's take a closer look at the main asset classes:

Stocks, also known as equities, represent ownership in a company. When you buy a stock, you're buying a small piece of that company and its future profits (or losses). Stocks have historically offered the highest potential for long-term growth, but they also come with the most volatility or short-term fluctuations in value. They're like the high-energy trail mix of your portfolio – they can give you a big boost, but can also lead to some jitters along the way.

Bonds are essentially loans that you make to a company or government. When you buy a bond, you're lending your money to the issuer in exchange for regular interest payments and the promise of getting your principal back at maturity. Bonds tend to be less volatile than stocks but also offer lower potential returns. They're like the sturdy hiking boots of your portfolio – they provide stability and support, but won't propel you forward as quickly as other options.

Cash and cash equivalents, such as money market funds, are the most conservative investments. They offer the lowest risk but also the lowest potential return. They're like the first aid kit of your portfolio – you hope you won't need to use them often, but they're essential to have for emergencies and short-term needs.

So how do you decide how much of each asset class to include in your portfolio? That's where asset allocation strategy comes in. Your ideal asset allocation will depend on several factors:

Your age and time horizon: Generally, the younger you are and the longer you have until retirement, the more risk you can afford to take. That's because you have more time to ride out market ups and downs. As you get closer to retirement, you may want to shift more of your portfolio into conservative investments to protect your nest egg.

Your risk tolerance: This is a measure of how much volatility you're comfortable with. Some people can stomach the rollercoaster ride of a stock-heavy portfolio, while others prefer a smoother journey. It's important to find a balance that lets you sleep at night while still achieving your long-term goals.

Your goals: What are you saving and investing for? Is your primary goal to grow your wealth as much as possible, or to generate a stable income stream in retirement? Different goals may call for different asset allocations.

One common approach is the "rule of 110" (or 120) for retirement. This rule of thumb suggests subtracting your age from 110 (or 120) to determine the percentage of stocks to hold in your portfolio. The rest would be allocated to bonds and cash. For example, a 40-year-old using the rule of 110 might have a portfolio of 70%

stocks (110 - 40 = 70) and 30% bonds and cash. Keep in mind this is a general guideline, not a hard and fast rule.

Another approach is to use target date funds, which automatically adjust your asset allocation based on your expected retirement year. These funds start with a higher allocation to stocks when you're younger, and gradually shift toward bonds as you near retirement. They're like having a trail guide who adjusts your pack based on the terrain ahead.

The key is to choose an asset allocation that aligns with your personal circumstances and stick with it over the long term, even when markets get volatile. Regularly rebalancing your portfolio (which we'll discuss later) can help you maintain your desired asset allocation as market conditions change.

In summary, asset allocation is all about finding the right balance of investments to help you reach your retirement goals while managing risk. It's a personal decision that depends on your age, risk tolerance, and objectives. By

65

understanding the characteristics of different asset classes and how they can work together, you can create a diversified portfolio that's built to weather the trails of the investment landscape.

Choosing the Right Investment Mix

Once you understand the concept of asset allocation, the next step is to choose the specific investments that will make up your portfolio. This is where you decide what goes into each compartment of your hiking pack – the exact brands of trail mix, types of hiking boots, and models of first aid kits that will serve you best on your journey.

The investment universe is vast and can be overwhelming, with countless mutual funds, exchange-traded funds (ETFs), individual stocks and bonds, and other securities to choose from. So how do you narrow it down and select the right mix for your retirement portfolio?

One important factor to consider is diversification. Just as you wouldn't want to pack only one flavor of trail mix, you don't want to put all your money in one or two investments. By spreading your money across different investments within each asset class, you can potentially reduce risk and smooth out returns over time.

For example, within the stock portion of your portfolio, you might want to include a mix of large, mid-size, and small company stocks, as well as both domestic and international stocks. Different sizes and types of companies tend to perform differently at different times, so owning a variety can provide balance.

Similarly, within the bond portion of your portfolio, you might include a mix of government bonds, corporate bonds, and municipal bonds with varying maturities and credit qualities. This diversification can help manage the risks specific to the bond market, such as interest rate risk and credit risk.

Another factor to consider is cost. Every investment has fees and expenses associated with it, whether it's the operating expenses of a mutual fund, the trading commissions for stocks, or the "expense ratios" of ETFs. These costs can eat into your returns over time, so it's important to be mindful of them when selecting investments.

In general, passively managed index funds and ETFs tend to have lower costs than actively managed funds. Index funds aim to match the performance of a specific market benchmark, such as the S&P 500 for large company stocks, by holding the same securities in the same proportions as the index. Actively managed funds, on the other hand, try to beat market returns and rely on professional fund managers to select investments, which can drive up costs.

Your specific investment choices will also depend on your personal preferences and circumstances. Some people enjoy researching individual stocks and bonds, while others prefer the simplicity and broad diversification of index funds. Your investment options may also be limited by what's available in your 401(k) or other retirement plan at work.

One approach is to start with a core of broad-based, low-cost index funds for each asset class. For example, you might select an S&P 500 index fund for large company stocks, a small-cap index fund for smaller companies, an international stock index fund, a total bond market index fund, and a money market or stable value fund for your cash allocation. From there, you can add in actively managed funds, sector-specific funds, or individual securities as complementary holdings.

Another option is to use all-in-one funds that provide a complete portfolio in a single investment. Target date funds, which we mentioned earlier, are one example. These funds automatically adjust your asset allocation over time based on your target retirement date. Another option is balanced funds, which maintain a fixed allocation to stocks and bonds (such as 60% stocks/40% bonds) and can provide a simple, one-stop-shop solution for your retirement portfolio.

The key is to choose a mix of investments that aligns with your overall asset allocation strategy and retirement goals. It's also important to periodically review your investment mix and make adjustments as needed. Your ideal portfolio at age 30 may no longer be a good fit at age 50, as your time horizon and risk tolerance change.

In summary, choosing the right investment mix is about selecting a diversified set of assets and securities within each asset class. Factors to consider include diversification, cost, and your personal preferences and circumstances. By building a well-rounded portfolio with a core of broad-based, low-cost options, and periodically reviewing and adjusting your mix, you can create a solid foundation for your retirement savings.

Rebalancing Your Portfolio

Picture this: You've packed your backpack for a long hike with the perfect balance of gear – just the right amount of food, water, clothing, and equipment to see you through. But as you trek along, you consume your supplies at different rates. Your trail mix disappears faster than your dried fruit, your water needs constant replenishing, and your first aid kit gets depleted from the occasional blister or scrape. Pretty soon, your once well-proportioned pack is out of balance, heavy on some items and light on others.

Your investment portfolio can experience a similar phenomenon over time. As market conditions change and your investments experience different rates of growth (or decline), your portfolio can drift away from your intended asset allocation. This is where rebalancing comes in – it's the process of periodically buying and selling assets to bring your portfolio back in line with your target allocation.

Let's look at a simple example. Say your target asset allocation is 60% stocks and 40% bonds. You start with $10,000, putting $6,000 in a stock index fund and $4,000 in a bond index fund. Over the next year, the stock market booms and your stock fund grows to $7,200, while your bond fund inches up to $4,200. Your portfolio is now worth $11,400, but it's drifted to 63% stocks and 37% bonds.

To rebalance back to your 60/40 target, you'd need to sell some stocks and buy more bonds. In this case, you'd sell $342 of your stock fund and use the proceeds to buy more of your bond fund. This would leave you with $6,858 in stocks (60% of $11,400) and $4,542 in bonds (40% of $11,400), restoring your intended balance.

Why bother with this periodic rebalancing? There are several key reasons:

Risk management: Your asset allocation is designed to manage risk by providing a balance between growth-oriented assets (like stocks) and more conservative, income-oriented assets (like bonds). By letting your portfolio drift too far from your intended allocation, you may be taking on more (or less) risk than you're comfortable with.

Buy low, sell high: Rebalancing naturally involves selling assets that have grown in value and buying assets that have lagged. In the example above, we sold stocks (which had gotten expensive) to buy more bonds (which were relatively cheaper). This disciplined approach can help you avoid the common pitfall of chasing performance and buying high and selling low.

Stick to your plan: Rebalancing is a way to enforce your original investment plan and avoid making emotional decisions based on market conditions. It can be tempting to let your winners ride and avoid the laggards, but this can lead to a portfolio that's out of sync with your goals and risk tolerance.

So how often should you rebalance? There's no one perfect answer, but many experts recommend rebalancing at least once a year, or whenever your portfolio drifts more than 5-10 percentage points from your target allocation.

Some retirement plans offer automatic rebalancing services that will adjust your holdings for you on a set schedule. If you're managing your own portfolio, you can set a calendar reminder to check your asset allocation periodically and make any necessary adjustments.

Another approach is to use rebalancing as an opportunity to make strategic shifts in your portfolio. For example, if you're nearing retirement and want to gradually reduce your risk exposure, you might use your annual rebalancing to incrementally shift more money from stocks to bonds.

It's important to note that rebalancing doesn't guarantee a profit or protect against a loss, especially in the short term. There may be times when your portfolio drifts far from your target allocation before you have a chance to rebalance, or when market conditions are so volatile that frequent rebalancing could do more harm than good. As with all aspects of investing, it's important to take a long-term view and avoid making knee-jerk reactions to short-term noise.

In summary, rebalancing is the process of periodically buying and selling assets to maintain your target asset allocation. It's an important tool for managing risk, avoiding emotional decision-making, and sticking to your long-term investment plan. By setting a regular rebalancing schedule or using automatic rebalancing services, you can help ensure that your portfolio stays on track to meet your retirement goals.

Chapter 6

Retirement Income Distribution Strategies

Sustainable Withdrawal Rates

You've spent decades diligently saving and investing for retirement, watching your nest egg grow. Now that retirement is here, it's time to shift gears and start drawing on those savings to support your lifestyle. But how much can you safely withdraw each year without running out of money? This is where understanding sustainable withdrawal rates becomes crucial.

Let's begin by defining what we mean by a sustainable withdrawal rate. In simple terms, it's the maximum percentage of your retirement savings that you can withdraw each year, adjusted for inflation, while still having a high probability of not outliving your money. It's like determining how much water you can draw from a well each day while ensuring the well doesn't run dry.

The most well-known research on this topic is the "Trinity study" or the "4% rule," which originated from a 1998 paper by three professors at Trinity University. They examined historical data to determine the success rates of different withdrawal rates over various time periods. Their key finding: a 4% initial withdrawal rate, adjusted each year for inflation, had a high success rate (above 95%) for portfolios with at least 50% stocks over 30 years.

Here's how the 4% rule works in practice: Let's say you retire with a portfolio of $1 million. In your first year of retirement, you withdraw 4% of your portfolio, or $40,000. The next year, you adjust this amount for inflation. If inflation was 2%, you'd withdraw $40,800 ($40,000 x 1.02). You continue this pattern each year, always adjusting the previous year's withdrawal by the rate of inflation.

The 4% rule is a useful starting point, but it's not a one-size-fits-all solution. There are several factors that can impact your personal sustainable withdrawal rate:

1. The length of your retirement: The longer your retirement horizon, the lower your sustainable withdrawal rate generally needs to be. If you retire early or have a long life expectancy, you may need to adjust downward from 4%.

2. Your asset allocation: The Trinity study assumed a portfolio of 50% stocks and 50% bonds. If your portfolio is more heavily weighted in stocks, you might be able to sustain a slightly higher withdrawal rate, but with more volatility. Conversely, a more conservative portfolio may require a lower withdrawal rate.

3. Market conditions in early retirement: As we'll discuss more in the next section, poor market returns in the early years of retirement can significantly impact the sustainability of your withdrawals. This is known as sequence of returns risk.

4. Flexibility in spending: The 4% rule assumes you'll increase your spending with inflation each year, come what may. In reality, most retirees have some flexibility to adjust spending if needed, especially on discretionary items. Being able to tighten the belt during down markets can significantly improve the sustainability of your withdrawals.

Given these variables, many financial planners now recommend starting with a lower initial withdrawal rate, such as 3% or 3.5%, particularly if you're retiring early or want a higher level of confidence your money will last.

Other strategies can also help stretch your retirement savings. One approach is to use a dynamic withdrawal strategy, where you adjust your withdrawals based on portfolio performance. For example, you might take a little less in down years and a little more in good years.

Another strategy is to segregate your portfolio into different "buckets" for different time horizons or purposes, such as a short-term bucket for immediate income needs and a long-term bucket that stays invested for growth.

It's also worth noting that your retirement income doesn't all have to come from your investment portfolio. Other sources, such as Social Security, pensions, rental income, or part-time work, can cover a portion of your expenses and reduce the strain on your portfolio.

The key thing to remember is that sustainable withdrawal rates are based on historical probabilities and assumptions. There's no guarantee that the future will look like the past, or that any particular withdrawal rate will work for your specific situation. That's why it's important to stay flexible, review your plan regularly, and make adjustments as your circumstances change.

Think of your withdrawal strategy as a compass guiding you through the wilderness of retirement. It provides direction, but you still need to navigate the actual terrain. By starting with a conservative withdrawal rate, building in flexibility, and diversifying your income sources, you can help ensure your retirement savings last as long as you need them.

Sequence of Returns Risk and Mitigation Strategies

In the journey of retirement, timing can be everything. Two retirees with identical portfolios and withdrawal strategies can have vastly different outcomes depending on when they retire. This is due to a phenomenon known as sequence of returns risk, and it's a crucial concept for retirees to understand.

Sequence of returns risk refers to the danger that your portfolio will experience poor investment returns in the early years of your retirement. This is problematic because you're simultaneously withdrawing money to live on, so you're taking a double hit – your portfolio value is declining from both poor returns and your withdrawals.

Here's an example to illustrate: Imagine two retirees, Alice and Bob, who each retire with a $1 million portfolio. They both plan to withdraw 4% of their initial portfolio value each year, adjusted for inflation. But there's a key difference: Alice retires at the start of a bull market, while Bob retires at the start of a bear market.

In Alice's first five years, her portfolio grows even after her withdrawals, thanks to strong market returns. This gives her portfolio a solid cushion to withstand any future downturns. In contrast, Bob's portfolio takes significant hits in his first five years. Even if he experiences the same strong returns as Alice later on, he's starting from a much lower base due to those early losses and withdrawals. As a result, Bob runs a higher risk of running out of money in his later retirement years.

This is the crux of the sequence of returns risk: it's not just the average return that matters, but the order in which those returns occur. Negative returns early in retirement, when your portfolio is at its largest, can have an outsized impact on your portfolio's longevity.

So what can retirees do to mitigate this risk? Here are several strategies:

1. Adjust your asset allocation: As you approach retirement, you might consider shifting a portion of your portfolio into more conservative investments, such as bonds or cash. This can help provide a buffer against market downturns in early retirement. However, you still want to keep a significant portion in growth-oriented assets to help keep pace with inflation over the long term.

2. Use a more conservative withdrawal rate: Instead of starting with a 4% withdrawal rate, consider starting with 3% or 3.5%, particularly if you're worried about a market downturn early in your retirement. This lower initial withdrawal gives your portfolio more breathing room.

3. Be flexible with your spending: Building some flexibility into your retirement budget is crucial. If you can cut back on discretionary spending during down markets, it reduces the stress on your portfolio and gives it more time to recover.

4. Consider a bucket strategy: One way to manage sequence risk is to divide your portfolio into different "buckets" for different time horizons. For example, you might have a cash bucket for your first year of expenses, a bond bucket for the next 4-9 years, and a stock bucket for long-term growth. This allows you to avoid selling stocks during a downturn, giving them time to recover.

5. Diversify your income sources: The more you can rely on non-portfolio income sources, such as Social Security, pensions, or annuities, the less you'll need to withdraw from your portfolio each year. This can be particularly helpful in mitigating the impact of poor returns early in retirement.

6. Use a dynamic withdrawal strategy: Instead of rigidly increasing your withdrawal by inflation each year, consider a more flexible approach that adjusts based on portfolio performance. For example, you might use a "guardrail" strategy where you increase your withdrawal by inflation in good years, but freeze or even reduce your withdrawal in down years.

7. Work part-time in early retirement: If you're able to generate even a small income from part-time work in the early years of retirement, it can make a big difference. Every dollar you earn is a dollar you don't have to withdraw from your portfolio.

Ultimately, managing sequence of returns risk is about building resilience into your retirement plan. It's preparing for the possibility of a stormy start to your retirement journey, knowing that you have the tools and flexibility to weather it.

Just as a hiker might carry extra supplies and have bailout routes planned in case of bad weather, a retiree should have contingency plans for poor market conditions. By using a conservative withdrawal rate, maintaining a balanced asset allocation, being flexible with your spending, and diversifying your income sources, you can significantly increase the odds that your retirement savings will last as long as you need them, no matter what sequence of returns the market deals you.

Annuities and Other Income-Generating Options

When it comes to retirement income, there's a psychological benefit to having a predictable "paycheck" that arrives each month, regardless of what the stock market is doing. This is where income-generating options like annuities, bond ladders, and dividend-paying stocks can play a role in a retirement income plan.

Let's start with annuities. An annuity is a contract between you and an insurance company, where you pay a lump sum or series of payments and in return, the insurer agrees to make periodic payments to you, either for a fixed term or for the rest of your life.

There are many types of annuities, but two main categories are immediate annuities and deferred annuities. With an immediate annuity, you start receiving payments right away. With a deferred annuity, your money grows tax-deferred until you choose to start taking withdrawals, typically in retirement.

One of the main advantages of annuities is that they can provide a guaranteed income stream for life, which can be a valuable hedge against the risk of outliving your money. With a lifetime immediate annuity, for example, you hand over a lump sum to an insurer, and they promise to pay you a fixed monthly amount for as long as you live, no matter how long that is.

However, this lifetime income guarantee comes at a cost. Annuities often have high fees, and you're typically giving up access to that lump sum. If you die early, the insurer usually keeps the remaining balance (unless you've opted for a "period certain" or "joint and survivor" payout). There's also the risk of the insurer going bust, though state insurance guarantee associations provide some protection.

Another potential drawback is that most annuities don't adjust for inflation. If you buy a fixed immediate annuity at age 65, the monthly payout you receive at age 85 will have significantly less purchasing power. Some annuities offer an inflation adjustment rider, but this comes at the cost of a lower initial payout.

Given these tradeoffs, annuities are often used as a piece of a retirement income plan, not the whole solution. For example, you might use a portion of your savings to buy an immediate annuity that covers your basic living expenses, while leaving the rest of your portfolio invested for growth to help keep pace with inflation.

Another option in the annuity space is a variable annuity with a guaranteed minimum withdrawal benefit (GMWB). These complex products let you invest in a portfolio of mutual funds within the annuity, while also providing a guaranteed lifetime withdrawal amount. However, they often come with very high costs that can eat into your returns.

Aside from annuities, another income-generating strategy is to build a ladder of bonds that mature at different dates. The idea is to divide your bond portfolio into equal portions that mature in different years, such as every year for the next 10 years. Each year, you live off the proceeds of the maturing bonds, and reinvest the money from the bonds at the end of the ladder into new 10-year bonds (or whatever your ladder length is). This strategy can provide a predictable income stream while also managing interest rate risk.

Dividend-paying stocks can also play a role in generating retirement income. Stocks that pay consistent, growing dividends can provide a source of cash flow that also has the potential to grow over time, helping to counter inflation. However, it's important to remember that dividends are never guaranteed and can be cut or eliminated if a company faces financial trouble. Dividend stocks should be seen as a long-term growth investment that happens to provide some income, not as a guaranteed income source.

Real estate can be another income-generating option, either through rental properties or REITs (real estate investment trusts). Rental properties can provide a regular income stream, potential for appreciation, and some tax benefits, but they also come with the responsibilities and risks of being a landlord. REITs allow you to invest in a diversified portfolio of income-producing real estate without the hands-on management, but like any stock investment, they come with market risk.

Ultimately, the right mix of income-generating options will depend on your individual financial situation, risk tolerance, and retirement goals. A financial advisor can help you sort through the options and create a personalized income plan.

The key is to build a diversified mix of income sources that can provide some stability and predictability, while also having the potential for growth to help combat inflation over the long term. By combining Social Security, any pension income, annuities, bond ladders, dividend stocks, and other investments, you can create a retirement "paycheck" that can help support you through the many years of your retirement journey.

Chapter 7

Exploring Additional Income Sources

Social Security Benefits Optimization

Social Security is a foundational piece of most Americans' retirement income plan. It's a program you pay into throughout your working life, and in return, you receive a monthly benefit in retirement that's adjusted for inflation each year. While it's not typically enough to fully fund a retirement on its own, it can provide a significant base of guaranteed income. And with some smart strategizing, you can maximize the benefits you receive.

The first key to optimizing your Social Security benefits is understanding how they're calculated. Your benefit is based on your 35 highest earning years. The Social Security Administration takes your earnings for each year, adjusts them for inflation, and then finds the average monthly amount. They then apply a formula to this average to determine your primary insurance amount (PIA), which is the benefit you'll receive if you start collecting at your full retirement age (FRA).

Your FRA is based on your birth year. For people born in 1960 or later, it's 67. For those born earlier, it's somewhere between 66 and 67. You can start taking benefits as early as age 62, but your benefit will be permanently reduced. On the flip side, for each year you delay past your FRA (up to age 70), your benefit will increase by 8%.

This leads to the central question in Social Security optimization: when should you start taking benefits? The answer depends on a variety of factors, including your health, your other sources of retirement income, and your family situation.

If you have reason to believe you'll have a shorter-than-average life expectancy, starting benefits early can make sense. Yes, your monthly checks will be smaller, but you'll receive more of them over your lifetime. On the other hand, if longevity runs in your family and you're in good health, delaying benefits can be a smart move. Those higher monthly checks can provide valuable protection against outliving your money.

Your other retirement resources also play a role. If you have ample savings and other sources of income, you may be able to afford to delay Social Security and let that benefit grow. But if Social Security will be your primary source of retirement income, you may need to start earlier to meet your cash flow needs.

For married couples, there are additional strategies to consider. In many cases, it makes sense for the higher earner to delay their benefit as long as possible, as this will maximize the survivor benefit for the longer-living spouse. The lower earner might start benefits earlier, providing some income in the meantime. Divorced individuals may also be able to claim benefits based on an ex-spouse's record if the marriage lasted 10 years or more.

Another factor to consider is your work plans in early retirement. If you start taking Social Security before your FRA and continue to work, your benefits may be temporarily reduced if your earnings exceed a certain threshold. Once you reach FRA, though, your benefit will be adjusted upward to account for these withheld benefits.

A crucial aspect of Social Security planning is understanding the tradeoffs involved. Starting early reduces your monthly benefit but increases the total number of checks you'll receive over a lifetime. Delaying increases your monthly benefit but means you'll receive fewer total checks. There's no universally "right" answer - it depends on your unique circumstances and priorities.

One helpful exercise is to calculate your "break even age" for different claiming strategies. This is the age at which the total benefits you've received from two different strategies will be equal. For example, if your FRA is 67 and you're deciding between starting benefits at 62 or 70, your breakeven age would be around 80. If you live past 80, delaying to 70 will result in more total benefits over your lifetime. But if you don't reach that age, starting at 62 would have been the better choice in hindsight.

Of course, we can't predict the future, and retirement planning always involves some uncertainty. That's why it's often wise to think in terms of probabilities and risk management rather than trying to find a "perfect" answer.

Social Security is also just one piece of the retirement puzzle, and your claiming strategy should be integrated with your overall financial plan. A financial advisor can help you navigate these complexities and make informed decisions based on your full financial picture.

Ultimately, the goal is to use Social Security as a tool to support the retirement lifestyle you want. By understanding how your benefit is calculated, considering your individual circumstances, and weighing the tradeoffs of different claiming strategies, you can make well-reasoned choices that optimize this valuable retirement resource.

Pension Plans and Lump-Sum Options

For those fortunate enough to have one, a pension can be a significant source of retirement income. A pension, also known as a defined benefit plan, is a retirement plan sponsored by an employer where the employee is promised a specified monthly benefit at retirement. This benefit is typically based on factors such as the employee's salary, age, and number of years of service.

Pensions used to be a common feature of American retirement, but they've become increasingly rare in the private sector. Many companies have shifted to defined contribution plans like 401(k)s, where the employee and/or employer contribute to an individual account, and the employee bears the investment risk. However, pensions are still common in the public sector, such as government jobs and some unionized industries.

If you have a pension, one of the key decisions you'll face at retirement is how to take your benefits. Most pensions offer a choice between a lifetime annuity (a set monthly payment for life) or a lump-sum payment.

The lifetime annuity provides a guaranteed income stream that you can't outlive. It's like a paycheck that keeps coming no matter how long you live. This can provide valuable peace of mind and financial security in retirement. If you're married, you'll typically have the option to choose a joint and survivor annuity, which continues payments (usually at a reduced rate) to your spouse after your death.

The lump-sum option, on the other hand, gives you a one-time payment of the total value of your pension. You then have to decide how to invest and manage that money to generate retirement income. The appeal of the lump sum is that you have control over the money. If you die early, any remaining balance can be passed on to your heirs. You also have the potential to grow the money if you invest it wisely.

So which option should you choose? As with most financial decisions, there's no one-size-fits-all answer. It depends on your individual circumstances and priorities.

One key factor to consider is your life expectancy. Pension annuities are calculated based on average life expectancies. If you're in good health and have reason to believe you'll live longer than average, the lifetime annuity can be a good deal. You'll likely receive more in total benefits over your lifetime than you would have with the lump sum. On the other hand, if you have health issues or a family history of shorter lifespans, the lump sum might be more attractive.

Your other retirement resources also play a role. If you have significant other savings and investments, you may be more comfortable taking the lump sum and managing it yourself. But if your pension is your primary source of retirement income, the guaranteed lifetime payments of an annuity can be more appealing.

Risk tolerance is another important consideration. With a lump sum, you're taking on the responsibility and the risks of investing that money. If you're comfortable making investment decisions and can handle some volatility in your returns, the lump sum can offer more flexibility and potential for growth. But if you prefer the certainty and simplicity of a set monthly check, the annuity may be a better fit.

It's also important to consider the financial stability of your employer. Pension benefits are insured by the Pension Benefit Guaranty Corporation (PBGC) up to certain limits, but if your employer goes bankrupt, you could still lose some of your benefits. If you have any concerns about your employer's long-term viability, that could tilt the scales toward taking the lump sum.

If you're married, it's crucial to involve your spouse in the decision. The choice between an annuity and a lump sum can have significant implications for your spouse's financial security, particularly if they're likely to outlive you.

One potential middle ground is to take the lump sum and use a portion of it to purchase an immediate annuity from an insurance company. This can provide a base of guaranteed lifetime income while still leaving some money under your control.

As with all retirement income decisions, it's wise to consult with a financial professional who can help you understand your options and make a choice that aligns with your overall financial plan. They can also help you compare the specific terms of your pension options, as the details can vary significantly from plan to plan.

Remember, a pension is a valuable asset, one that can provide significant financial security in retirement. By carefully considering your options and making an informed decision, you can make the most of this important retirement resource.

Reverse Mortgages and Home Equity

For many retirees, their home is their most valuable asset. But traditionally, this asset has been difficult to tap for retirement income unless you were willing to sell the home and downsize or rent. This is where reverse mortgages come in. A reverse mortgage is a financial product that allows homeowners aged 62 and older to convert a portion of their home equity into cash without having to sell their home or take on monthly mortgage payments.

Here's how it works: The homeowner takes out a loan against the value of their home. But unlike a traditional mortgage, they don't have to make monthly payments. Instead, the loan balance grows over time, and the full amount doesn't come due until the homeowner dies, sells the home, or moves out for more than 12 months.

The amount you can borrow depends on your age, the value of your home, and current interest rates. The older you are and the more valuable your home, the more you can typically borrow. You can receive the money as a lump sum, as monthly payments, as a line of credit that you draw upon as needed, or a combination of these.

The most common type of reverse mortgage is the Home Equity Conversion Mortgage (HECM), which is insured by the Federal Housing Administration (FHA). These loans have several important consumer protections. For example, you can never owe more than the value of your home, even if your loan balance grows to exceed that amount. You also have the right to stay in your home as long as you keep up with property taxes, insurance, and maintenance, even if you use up all your loan proceeds.

Reverse mortgages can be a valuable tool for generating retirement income, but they also have significant costs and risks to consider. The upfront costs can be substantial, including lender fees, FHA insurance premiums, and closing costs. These costs are typically rolled into the loan balance, so you're not paying them out of pocket, but they do reduce the amount of equity you can access.

Interest also accrues on the loan balance over time, and since you're not making payments, this interest compounds. This means your debt grows faster the longer you have the loan.

There's also the risk that you could use up all your loan proceeds too quickly and not have enough left for future needs. If you take the money as a lump sum and spend it all, you've essentially used up a significant asset that could have provided ongoing income.

Another potential downside is that a reverse mortgage can complicate matters for your heirs. When you die, your heirs will need to repay the loan if they want to keep the home. This typically means selling the home to pay off the debt, unless they have other funds available.

Despite these drawbacks, a reverse mortgage can be a useful financial tool in certain situations. For example, if you have significant home equity but limited other retirement savings, a reverse mortgage can provide a source of income to supplement Social Security and any other income sources. It can also serve as a financial backup plan - a line of credit that you can tap if unexpected expenses arise.

A reverse mortgage can also be used strategically as part of a broader retirement income plan. For example, by tapping home equity, you may be able to delay claiming

Social Security, allowing your benefit to grow. Or you could use reverse mortgage funds to pay for long-term care expenses, preserving other assets.

However, a reverse mortgage should generally be seen as a last resort, not a first choice. Before considering a reverse mortgage, it's important to explore other options, such as downsizing, selling your home and renting, or traditional home equity loans or lines of credit.

If you do decide to pursue a reverse mortgage, it's crucial to do your homework. Understand all the costs and risks involved, and compare offers from multiple lenders. Federal regulations require all borrowers to go through a counseling session with a HUD-approved counselor before taking out a HECM reverse mortgage, which can help you understand the implications.

It's also wise to involve your family in the decision, especially if you hope to leave your home to your heirs. Make sure they understand how the loan works and what it will mean for them.

Remember, your home is not just a financial asset - it's also a place of comfort, security, and memories. Any decision to tap into your home equity should be made carefully, with a full understanding of the trade-offs involved.

In the right circumstances, a reverse mortgage can be a valuable tool for supplementing retirement income and providing financial flexibility. But it's not a decision to be made lightly. As with all financial matters in retirement, it's best to consult with a trusted financial advisor who can help you weigh your options and make a choice that aligns with your overall financial goals and values.

Chapter 8

Minimizing Taxes in Retirement

Tax-Efficient Withdrawal Strategies

Picture your retirement savings as a garden, filled with different types of plants. Some of these plants (like your 401(k) or traditional IRA) have grown tax-deferred, meaning you didn't pay taxes on the money you put in or the growth along the way. Others (like Roth IRAs) were planted with after-tax dollars, but they grow tax-free. Still others (like taxable investment accounts) are like perennials that you have to prune (pay taxes on) each year.

When it comes time to harvest this garden for retirement income, the order and manner in which you pick the fruits can have a big impact on your total tax bill. Just as a smart gardener thinks strategically about what to harvest when for maximum yield and sustainability, a smart retiree thinks strategically about drawing down their assets in a tax-efficient manner.

The traditional approach to retirement withdrawals is to start with taxable accounts, then move on to tax-deferred accounts, and finally tap tax-free accounts like Roth IRAs. The thinking behind this sequence is to let the tax-advantaged accounts continue to grow for as long as possible.

However, this approach isn't always optimal from a tax perspective. Remember, when you take money out of those tax-deferred accounts, it's taxed as ordinary income. If all of your retirement savings is in traditional 401(k)s and IRAs, you could find yourself bumped into a higher tax bracket in retirement, especially once you factor in required minimum distributions (RMDs) that kick in at age 72.

This is where strategic tax planning comes in. The goal is to mix and match your withdrawals from different account types to keep your overall tax bill as low as possible over your retirement years. It's like picking a balanced bouquet from your garden, rather than just clear-cutting one section at a time.

One strategy is to take advantage of lower-income years (especially early in retirement before Social Security and RMDs kick in) to withdraw some money from your tax-deferred accounts. You pay the taxes now, but at a potentially lower rate than you would later. You can then move this money into a Roth IRA (if you're under the income limit for Roth contributions) or a taxable account, providing a source of tax-free or more tax-favored income for later in retirement.

Another approach is to draw simultaneously from multiple account types each year, using tax projections to determine the optimal mix. For example, you might take just enough from your tax-deferred accounts to "fill up" your current tax bracket, then draw the rest of your income needs from taxable or Roth accounts.

Taxable accounts offer some unique tax planning opportunities. When you sell investments in these accounts, you pay capital gains tax on the growth, but the tax rate is determined by how long you've held the investment. If you've held it for more than a year, you qualify for long-term capital gains rates, which are lower than ordinary income rates for most people. You can also use tax-loss harvesting in taxable accounts - selling investments that have gone down in value to offset capital gains or ordinary income.

Your specific mix will depend on factors like your tax bracket, your account balances, your other sources of income, and your legacy goals. The key is to be proactive and strategic, rather than just following a default withdrawal order.

Of course, taxes are just one piece of the retirement income puzzle. You also need to consider factors like your cash flow needs, your investment mix, and your risk tolerance. And tax laws can change over time, so it's important to stay flexible and review your plan regularly.

This is where working with a financial advisor and/or tax professional can be invaluable. They can help you create a comprehensive retirement income plan that takes into account all of these moving parts. They can run projections to show you the tax implications of different withdrawal strategies and help you adapt your plan as your circumstances change.

Ultimately, the goal of tax-efficient withdrawal strategies is to help your retirement savings last as long as possible while supporting the lifestyle you want. By being strategic about what you harvest from your retirement garden and when, you can potentially reduce your total tax bill, stretch your savings further, and create a more sustainable retirement income stream. It's an extra layer of planning, but one that can yield significant benefits over the course of a long retirement.

Roth Conversions and Tax Diversification

Continuing with our gardening analogy, imagine if you could transform some of those tax-deferred plants in your retirement garden into tax-free ones. That's essentially what a Roth conversion allows you to do. You take money out of your traditional IRA, pay the taxes on it now, and plant it in a Roth IRA where it can grow tax-free and be withdrawn tax-free in retirement.

Why would you choose to pay taxes now instead of deferring them into the future? There are several potential benefits:

1. You believe you will be in a higher tax bracket in retirement than you are now. By paying the taxes at your current, lower rate, you can save on taxes in the long run.

2. You want to reduce your future required minimum distributions (RMDs). Roth IRAs are not subject to

RMDs during the original owner's lifetime, so converting can give you more flexibility in retirement.

3. You want to leave a tax-free inheritance to your beneficiaries. While beneficiaries must take distributions from inherited Roth IRAs, those distributions are typically tax-free.

4. You want to diversify your tax situation in retirement. Having some money in Roth accounts gives you a source of tax-free income to mix with your taxable and tax-deferred income sources.

That last point is key. Just as diversifying your investments can help manage risk, diversifying your retirement accounts from a tax perspective can give you more flexibility and control over your tax situation in retirement.

Think of it like planting different varieties of the same vegetable in your garden. They might require slightly different care and produce fruit at different times, but having that variety makes your garden more resilient and provides a longer harvest season.

The same principle applies to your retirement savings. If all of your savings is in tax-deferred accounts, you're limited in how you can manage your taxable income in retirement. But if you have a mix of taxable, tax-deferred, and Roth accounts, you have more levers to pull in terms of managing your tax bracket, your cash flow, and your legacy planning.

So how do Roth conversions fit into this strategy? They're a way to gradually shift some of your savings from tax-deferred to tax-free over time. The process works like this:

1. You transfer some money from your traditional IRA to a Roth IRA. The amount you convert is added to your taxable income for the year.

2. You pay the taxes on the converted amount. It's important to pay these taxes from outside funds if

possible, rather than withholding them from the converted amount, to maximize the amount that's growing tax-free.

3. The converted money can now grow tax-free in the Roth IRA, and you can withdraw it tax-free in retirement (as long as you meet certain conditions).

You can do partial conversions over multiple years to spread out the tax impact. For example, you might convert just enough each year to "fill up" your current tax bracket without spilling into the next one.

You can also be strategic about the timing of your conversions. For instance, you might choose to do more conversions in a year when your income is lower (perhaps due to a gap in employment or a large deduction), or in a year when tax rates are lower due to legislative changes.

It's important to note that Roth conversions aren't right for everyone. If you expect to be in a lower tax bracket in retirement than you are now, you may be better off keeping your money in tax-deferred accounts and paying the taxes later. Conversions can also be costly in the short term, so you need to have the funds available to pay the tax bill.

There are also some technical rules around Roth conversions, such as the five-year rule for withdrawals and the impact on things like the taxation of Social Security benefits and Medicare premiums. This is where working with a financial advisor and/or tax professional is crucial to ensure you're considering all the angles.

Ultimately, Roth conversions are a tool for tax diversification and long-term tax planning. By strategically moving some of your savings into Roth accounts over time, you can potentially reduce your total lifetime tax bill, gain more flexibility in retirement, and create a more tax-efficient legacy for your beneficiaries. It's a complex decision with many moving parts, but for some retirees, it can be a powerful way to optimize their retirement garden.

Charitable Giving and Estate Planning

While much of retirement planning focuses on ensuring you have enough money to live comfortably, it's also important to think about the legacy you want to leave. For many people, this includes supporting the causes and organizations they care about through charitable giving. Strategic charitable giving can not only benefit the charities you support, but it can also play a role in your overall tax and estate planning.

One straightforward way to give to charity is through direct cash donations. These donations are typically tax-deductible if you itemize your deductions. However, with the standard deduction now higher due to the Tax Cuts and Jobs Act, fewer people are itemizing. This means that your charitable giving may not directly impact your taxes unless your total itemized deductions exceed the standard deduction threshold.

However, there are strategies that can allow you to still gain tax benefits from your charitable giving. One is bunching donations. Instead of giving a smaller amount each year, you give a larger amount in one year to exceed the standard deduction threshold and itemize your deductions that year. Then, you take the standard deduction in the off years. This can allow you to get a tax benefit for your giving while still supporting your chosen charities regularly.

Another strategy is donating appreciated assets, such as stocks, instead of cash. When you donate an appreciated asset that you've held for more than a year directly to a charity, you can deduct the full fair market value of the asset without having to pay capital gains tax on the appreciation. This can be a particularly effective strategy if you have highly appreciated assets that would trigger a large capital gain if sold.

Retirement accounts can also play a role in charitable giving. If you're 70½ or older, you can make qualified charitable distributions (QCDs) of up to $100,000 per year directly from your IRA to charity. These distributions count towards your required minimum distribution (RMD) but are not included in your taxable income. This can be a way to support charity while also managing the taxable income from your RMDs.

For those with larger estates, more advanced charitable giving strategies can come into play. These might include:

- Charitable remainder trusts, where you place assets into a trust that pays you an income stream for a set period, with the remainder going to charity at the end of the term.

- Charitable lead trusts, where the trust pays income to charity for a set period, with the remainder going to your beneficiaries at the end of the term.

- Donor-advised funds, where you make a contribution to a fund and then recommend grants from the fund to your chosen charities over time.

These strategies can provide tax benefits while also allowing you to support charity and pass assets to your heirs in a controlled manner.

Of course, charitable giving is just one aspect of estate planning. A comprehensive estate plan also includes things like wills, trusts, powers of attorney, and health care directives. The goal is to ensure your assets are distributed according to your wishes and your loved ones are taken care of after you're gone.

From a tax perspective, estate planning often focuses on minimizing estate taxes. The federal estate tax only applies to very large estates (over $12.92 million per individual in 2023), but some states have lower thresholds. Strategies for minimizing estate taxes can include:

- Making annual gifts to heirs during your lifetime to reduce the size of your taxable estate.

- Using irrevocable trusts to remove assets from your estate while still providing for your heirs.

- Ensuring your beneficiary designations on retirement accounts and life insurance policies are up to date, as these assets pass outside of your estate.

- Taking advantage of the unlimited marital deduction to pass assets to a spouse tax-free.

- Using the generation-skipping transfer tax exemption to pass assets directly to grandchildren or great-grandchildren.

Estate planning is a complex area that involves navigating a web of tax rules, legal requirements, and family dynamics. It's crucial to work with experienced estate planning professionals, such as an estate planning attorney and a financial advisor with experience in this area, to create a plan that meets your unique goals and circumstances.

Ultimately, charitable giving and estate planning are about more than just taxes. They're about your values, your legacy, and the impact you want to have on the world and the people you care about. By integrating these considerations into your overall retirement plan, you can create a more holistic and meaningful vision for your golden years - one that encompasses not just your own financial security, but the well-being of the causes and people that matter most to you.

Chapter 9

Creating a Comprehensive Retirement Plan

Putting the Pieces Together

Throughout our journey into retirement planning, we've explored many different pieces of the puzzle - from understanding your retirement income needs and maximizing your savings, to creating an investment strategy and managing taxes. Each of these pieces is important in its own right, but the real power comes when you put them all together into a comprehensive retirement plan.

Think of it like building a house. You need a strong foundation (your retirement savings), sturdy walls (your investment strategy), a watertight roof (your risk management plan), and a well-designed interior (your retirement income and tax strategies). Each component plays a crucial role, but it's only when they all work together that you have a complete and functional home.

So how do you go about putting the pieces of your retirement plan together? It starts with having a clear vision of what you want your retirement to look like. What are your goals and aspirations? Do you want to travel the world, spend more time with family, pursue a passion project, or start a new business? Your retirement vision will serve as the blueprint for your plan.

Next, you need to assess where you stand today. This means taking a comprehensive inventory of your current financial situation, including your income, expenses, assets, liabilities, and insurance coverage. This will give you a clear starting point and help you identify any gaps or areas that need attention.

From there, you can start putting the core components of your plan in place:

1. Your retirement income strategy: Based on your estimated expenses and desired lifestyle, how much income will you need in retirement? Where will this income come from - Social Security, pensions, rental income, part-time work, your investment portfolio? How will you structure your withdrawals to ensure a sustainable income stream?

2. Your investment plan: How will you allocate your assets across different investment types to balance growth and risk management? What's your target asset allocation, and how will you adjust it as you move closer to and through retirement?

3. Your tax plan: How can you optimize your tax situation in retirement? What's your strategy for withdrawals from your various accounts (taxable, tax-deferred, tax-free) to minimize your tax bill? Are there proactive strategies you can employ, such as Roth conversions?

4. Your risk management plan: How will you protect your retirement assets and income from key risks such as market downturns, inflation, health care costs, and longevity? What insurance coverages and contingency funds do you need in place?

5. Your estate plan: How do you want your assets to be managed and distributed after your death? What legal documents (wills, trusts, powers of attorney) and beneficiary designations do you need to ensure your wishes are carried out?

As you develop each component of your plan, it's important to consider how they interact and influence each other. For example, your investment strategy will impact your income strategy, which in turn affects your tax planning. Your risk management approach (such as the types of insurance you choose) will impact your expenses and cash flow.

This is where the real value of comprehensive planning comes in - it allows you to see the big picture and make strategic decisions that optimize your overall financial situation. It's not just about having a collection of separate strategies, but about having an integrated plan where all the pieces work together seamlessly.

Of course, creating a comprehensive retirement plan is not a one-time event. Your plan should be a living document that evolves with you over time. As your life circumstances change - a new grandchild arrives, you receive an inheritance, your health status changes - your plan should be updated to reflect your new reality.

Think of your retirement plan as your roadmap for navigating the financial landscape of your later years. It provides direction and guidance, but it also allows for detours and course corrections as needed. The key is to have a well-thought-out plan in place, to review it regularly, and to make informed adjustments along the way.

Putting the pieces of your retirement plan together can seem daunting at first, but it's a vital step in ensuring a secure and fulfilling retirement. By taking a comprehensive, holistic approach - one that encompasses all the key elements of your financial life - you can create a robust plan that will guide you through the challenges and opportunities of this exciting new chapter.

Stress-Testing Your Plan and Preparing for the Unexpected

Picture this: You've spent months, maybe even years, carefully crafting your retirement plan. You've considered your income needs, optimized your investment strategy, and put contingencies in place for healthcare costs and other risks. Your plan looks perfect on paper - but will it hold up in the real world?

This is where stress-testing comes in. Just as engineers put new designs through rigorous tests to see how they perform under pressure, you need to put your retirement plan through some hypothetical challenges to see how resilient it is.

What kind of scenarios should you test for? Here are a few key ones:

1. Market downturns: How would your plan fare if there was a significant and prolonged market downturn early in your retirement? This is the concept of sequence of returns risk that we discussed earlier. Stress-test your plan with different market scenarios, such as a 20% or 30% drop in the first year of retirement, to see how it impacts your long-term income sustainability.

2. Inflation spikes: Your plan likely incorporates an assumed inflation rate, but what if inflation spikes higher than expected? Test your plan with different inflation scenarios to see how it affects your purchasing power over time.

3. Longevity: What if you or your spouse live much longer than expected? Stress-test your plan to see if it can sustain your income needs to age 90, 95, or even 100.

4. Healthcare costs: Healthcare is one of the biggest and most unpredictable expenses in retirement. Consider scenarios where your healthcare costs are significantly higher than anticipated, whether due to a chronic condition or the need for long-term care.

5. Policy changes: What if there are significant changes to key policies that affect your retirement, such as Social Security benefits, tax rates, or Medicare provisions? See how your plan holds up under different policy scenarios.

The goal of stress-testing isn't to make you feel pessimistic or discouraged about your plan - it's to help you identify potential vulnerabilities and make your plan more robust. If your plan can weather these hypothetical storms, you'll have greater confidence in its ability to carry you through a long and fulfilling retirement.

So how do you actually go about stress-testing your plan? One way is to use financial planning software or calculators that allow you to input different scenarios and see the outcomes. Many of these tools use Monte Carlo simulations, which run your plan through hundreds or thousands of different return scenarios to see the probability of success.

Another approach is to work with a financial advisor who can help you model different scenarios and make adjustments to your plan as needed. They can bring a valuable outside perspective and help you think through potential risks and contingencies you may not have considered.

As you stress-test your plan, you may identify areas that need shoring up. Perhaps you need to increase your savings rate, adjust your asset allocation, or purchase additional insurance coverage. You may also identify some "levers" you can pull in the event of a downturn or unexpected expense, such as reducing discretionary spending or downsizing your home.

The key is to have a plan B (and possibly C and D) in place before you need it. This is where the concept of adaptive planning comes in. Rather than having a rigid, set-it-and-forget-it plan, an adaptive plan has built-in flexibility to respond to changing circumstances.

For example, your plan might include decision rules for how you'll adjust your spending in response to market conditions. If your portfolio drops by a certain percentage, you'll reduce your discretionary spending by a corresponding amount until the market recovers. Or your plan might outline a phased retirement approach, where you gradually reduce your work hours over a few years rather than abruptly stopping, allowing you to adapt to your new retirement lifestyle and budget.

No matter how well you plan, the reality is that life is full of surprises. The best retirement plan is one that is not only comprehensive and well-thought-out but also adaptable and resilient. By stress-testing your plan and building in contingencies and flexibility, you can approach retirement with greater confidence, knowing that you're prepared for whatever comes your way.

Remember, your retirement plan is not a static document - it's a dynamic tool that should evolve with you over time. Regular stress-testing and review should be a part of your ongoing retirement planning process. As you encounter new challenges and opportunities in retirement, your plan should adapt and grow with you, providing a stable foundation for this exciting new chapter of life.

The Importance of Working with Financial Professionals

Throughout our exploration of retirement planning, a recurring theme has emerged: it's complex. From understanding the intricacies of investment strategies and tax laws, to navigating the ever-changing landscape of retirement policies and products, there's a lot to keep up with. And the stakes are high - the decisions you make about your retirement can have a profound impact on your financial security and quality of life for decades to come.

This is where working with financial professionals can be invaluable. Just as you wouldn't try to diagnose a serious medical condition on your own, or represent yourself in a high-stakes legal case, managing your retirement finances is an area where expert guidance can make a world of difference.

So what types of financial professionals might you consider working with? Here are a few key players:

1. Financial Advisors: A financial advisor is a broad term that can encompass many different types of professionals, from investment managers to comprehensive financial planners. The key is to find an advisor who is a fiduciary, meaning they are legally and ethically bound to act in your best interests. A good financial advisor will take the time to understand your unique circumstances, goals, and risk tolerance, and help you create a customized plan to achieve your objectives. They can provide valuable guidance on investment strategies, retirement income planning, tax optimization, and more.

2. Certified Public Accountants (CPAs): CPAs are experts in taxation and accounting. They can help you navigate the complex world of tax planning, both in the lead up to and during retirement. This might include strategies for minimizing your tax liability, optimizing your withdrawals from various accounts, and charitable giving. They can also help you with budgeting, record-keeping, and preparing your tax returns.

3. Estate Planning Attorneys: Estate planning is a crucial component of a comprehensive retirement plan. An estate planning attorney can help you create legal documents such as wills, trusts, powers of attorney, and health care directives to ensure your wishes are carried out and your assets are protected. They can also help you navigate complex issues such as probate, business succession planning, and special needs trusts.

4. Insurance Professionals: Insurance is a key tool for managing risk in retirement. An insurance professional can help you assess your insurance needs and choose the right policies to protect your health, your income, your assets, and your legacy. This might include health insurance, long-term care insurance, life insurance, and annuities.

When choosing financial professionals to work with, it's important to do your due diligence. Look for professionals who are properly credentialed, experienced, and reputable in their field. Ask about their fees and how they are compensated - you want to ensure their incentives are aligned with your best interests.

It's also important to find professionals who you feel comfortable working with and who communicate in a way that you understand. Your retirement plan is deeply personal, and you should feel confident that your advisors "get" you and your unique situation.

But perhaps the most important reason to work with financial professionals is that they can provide an objective, outside perspective. When it comes to our own money, it's easy to get emotional or fall prey to behavioral biases. We might avoid making difficult decisions, or react impulsively to market movements. A good financial advisor can help you stay focused on your long-term plan and make rational, informed decisions, even in the face of short-term noise or challenges.

Of course, working with financial professionals doesn't mean abdicating control over your retirement planning. Ultimately, it's your money and your life, and you need to be an active participant in the process. But think of your advisors as your team of expert guides, helping you navigate the wilderness of retirement planning.

In practice, this might look like meeting with your financial advisor regularly to review your plan and make adjustments as needed. It could involve working with your CPA each year to optimize your tax strategy, or meeting with your estate planning attorney to update your documents after a major life event. The key is to establish and maintain these relationships over time, so that you have a trusted network of experts to turn to as your needs and circumstances evolve.

Retirement planning is not a solo journey - it's a collaborative process that involves marshaling the expertise and resources of multiple professionals. By building a team of trusted advisors, and leveraging their knowledge and guidance, you can create a more robust, comprehensive, and effective retirement plan - one that will help you navigate the challenges and opportunities of this exciting new chapter with confidence and peace of mind.

Chapter 10

Enjoying Your Retirement

Retirement Lifestyle Planning (Housing, Travel, Budgeting)

Picture retirement as the beginning of a new and exciting chapter in the book of your life. Just as you wouldn't start a new chapter without some idea of the setting, characters, and plot, you don't want to embark on retirement without a vision for what you want this phase of your life to look like. This is where retirement lifestyle planning comes in - it's the process of designing and preparing for the kind of life you want to lead in retirement.

Let's start with one of the most fundamental aspects of your retirement lifestyle: housing. Where and how you choose to live in retirement can have a profound impact on your quality of life, as well as your financial situation. Many retirees opt to stay in their current home, especially if it's fully paid off and holds sentimental value. This can provide a sense of familiarity and stability in a time of transition.

However, your current home may not be the best fit for your retirement needs and desires. Perhaps you have more space than you need now that your children are grown, and you'd prefer a smaller, more manageable home. Or maybe you live in an area with a high cost of living, and relocating to a more affordable city or state could significantly stretch your retirement dollars. Some retirees choose to downsize to a condo or apartment to reduce maintenance responsibilities, while others opt for a retirement community that offers amenities and social opportunities.

Another housing option to consider is a reverse mortgage. As we discussed earlier, this is a financial product that allows you to tap into your home equity to supplement your retirement income. While it's not the right choice for everyone, a reverse mortgage can be a way to stay in your home while also freeing up some additional cash flow.

No matter what housing path you choose, the key is to think ahead and make proactive choices. Don't wait until you're in the midst of retirement to realize that your home no longer suits your needs or that your housing costs are unsustainable. Start exploring your options early, and consider not just your current situation but also your potential future needs, such as accessibility modifications for aging in place.

Next, let's talk about travel. For many people, retirement is the time to finally take those trips they've been dreaming of for years. With more time and flexibility, retirement can be the perfect opportunity to explore new places, visit far-flung family and friends, or even live abroad for a period of time.

However, travel can also be a significant expense in retirement. When planning your retirement lifestyle, it's important to be realistic about your travel goals and to build the associated costs into your budget. This might mean prioritizing certain trips over others, finding ways to travel more affordably (such as through house swapping or traveling during off-seasons), or adjusting other areas of your spending to accommodate your travel desires.

One approach is to create a separate travel fund as part of your retirement savings. Throughout your working years, you can allocate a portion of your savings specifically for future travel. This way, you'll have dedicated resources to fund your adventures without having to dip into your core retirement income.

Finally, let's discuss the overarching topic of budgeting in retirement. Regardless of your specific retirement lifestyle choices, having a clear and realistic budget is essential. Your budget is the tool that will help you align your spending with your priorities and ensure that your money lasts as long as you need it to.

Start by estimating your retirement income from all sources - Social Security, pensions, retirement account withdrawals, rental income, part-time work, etc. Then, list out your anticipated expenses, being as specific as possible. Don't forget to account for one-time or irregular expenses, such as home repairs or replacing a vehicle.

Once you have your income and expense projections, look for any gaps or misalignments. Are your projected expenses exceeding your income? Are you allocating your money in a way that reflects your values and priorities? You may need to make some adjustments, such as reducing certain expenses, finding ways to increase your income, or shifting your spending to better match your goals.

Remember, your retirement budget is not a static document - it's a dynamic tool that should be reviewed and updated regularly. As your circumstances and priorities shift over the course of your retirement, your budget should evolve accordingly.

The key to successful retirement lifestyle planning is to start early, be proactive, and remain flexible. By thinking ahead about your housing, travel, and budgeting needs and desires, and by making informed choices that align with your values and resources, you can design a retirement lifestyle that is both fulfilling and sustainable over the long term. Like any good chapter in a book, your retirement should be a time of growth, adventure, and enjoyment - and with careful planning, it can be just that.

Maintaining Physical and Mental Health in Retirement

While much of retirement planning focuses on financial health - saving enough, investing wisely, creating a sustainable income stream - it's equally important to plan for your physical and mental health in retirement. After all, what good is a robust retirement fund if you don't have the health and vitality to enjoy it?

Let's start with physical health. As we age, it's natural for our bodies to change and for certain health risks to increase. However, there's a lot we can do to promote healthy aging and maintain our physical wellbeing in retirement.

One of the most important steps is to stay active. Regular physical activity has been shown to reduce the risk of chronic diseases, improve mental health, and even extend longevity. Aim for at least 150 minutes of moderate aerobic activity or 75 minutes of vigorous aerobic activity per week, along with muscle-strengthening activities at least twice a week. This can include activities like walking, swimming, cycling, dancing, or strength training.

Of course, it's important to choose activities that you enjoy and that suit your fitness level. If you haven't been active in a while, start slowly and gradually build up your endurance and strength. Consider working with a personal trainer or joining a class specifically designed for seniors to learn proper techniques and avoid injury.

In addition to exercise, a healthy diet is crucial for maintaining physical health in retirement. Focus on eating a variety of nutrient-dense foods, including fruits, vegetables, whole grains, lean proteins, and healthy fats. Limit your intake of processed foods, saturated fats, and added sugars. Staying hydrated is also important, so aim to drink plenty of water throughout the day.

Regular health check-ups are another key component of maintaining physical health in retirement. Be sure to schedule annual physicals, as well as recommended screenings such as colonoscopies, mammograms, and prostate exams. Don't hesitate to discuss any health concerns or changes with your doctor, no matter how minor they may seem.

It's also important to manage any chronic health conditions, such as diabetes, hypertension, or arthritis. This may involve taking medications as prescribed, monitoring your symptoms, and making lifestyle changes such as adjusting your diet or activity level. Working closely with your healthcare team can help you keep your conditions under control and maintain the best possible quality of life.

Now, let's talk about mental health. Retirement can bring many joys and opportunities, but it can also be a time of significant transition and adjustment. It's not uncommon for retirees to experience feelings of loss, boredom, or isolation, especially in the early stages of retirement.

One of the best ways to promote mental health in retirement is to stay socially connected. Maintain relationships with family and friends, and make an effort to build new social connections. Join clubs or groups that align with your interests, volunteer in your community, or take classes to learn new skills and meet new people. Regular social interaction can help ward off feelings of loneliness and depression, and provide a sense of purpose and belonging.

Engaging in mentally stimulating activities is also important for cognitive health. Reading, puzzles, learning a new language, playing an instrument - these kinds of activities can help keep your mind sharp and may even reduce the risk of cognitive decline. Challenging your brain with new experiences and information helps to build cognitive reserve, which can provide a buffer against age-related mental changes.

Stress management is another crucial aspect of mental health in retirement. While retirement can eliminate some stressors, like workplace pressures, it can also introduce new ones, such as financial worries or caregiving responsibilities. Developing healthy coping mechanisms, such as meditation, deep breathing, or talking with a trusted friend or therapist, can help you navigate stressful situations more effectively.

Finally, don't underestimate the power of a positive attitude. Studies have shown that having a positive outlook on aging can actually lead to better health outcomes and greater longevity. Instead of focusing on the limitations or challenges of aging, try to embrace the opportunities and joys that this stage of life can bring.

Remember, maintaining physical and mental health in retirement is an ongoing process. It requires intentional effort and proactive choices, but the payoff - a healthier, happier, and more fulfilling retirement - is well worth it. By making your health a priority and taking steps to nurture your physical and mental wellbeing, you can ensure that your retirement years are not just long, but also vibrant and enriching.

Finding Purpose, Fulfillment, and Leaving a Legacy

In the depths of our hearts, we all yearn for a life that matters - a life filled with meaning, purpose, and the sense that we've made a difference in the world. This desire doesn't fade as we age; if anything, it intensifies as we enter retirement and reflect on the legacy we want to leave behind.

Finding purpose and fulfillment in retirement is a deeply personal journey. What brings meaning to one person's life may be entirely different from what brings meaning to another's. The key is to engage in a process of self-reflection and exploration to uncover what matters most to you.

Start by thinking about your values - the fundamental beliefs that guide your decisions and actions. What principles do you hold most dear? Is it compassion, creativity, learning, service, or something else entirely?

Clarifying your values can provide a roadmap for finding fulfillment in retirement.

Next, consider your passions and interests. What activities make you lose track of time, bring you joy, or ignite your curiosity? Perhaps it's gardening, woodworking, writing, or volunteering at a local animal shelter. Retirement provides a unique opportunity to dive deeper into these passions, or to explore new ones you've always wanted to try.

For many retirees, a sense of purpose comes from contributing to something larger than themselves. This might involve volunteering for a cause you care about, mentoring younger generations in your field of expertise, or participating in community service projects. Giving back not only benefits others, but it can also provide a profound sense of meaning and connection.

Some retirees find fulfillment in paid work, either by turning a hobby into a small business, consulting part-time in their former field, or embarking on an entirely new career path. The key is to choose work that aligns with your values and passions, rather than working solely for financial gain.

Lifelong learning is another pathway to purpose in retirement. Taking classes, attending workshops, or pursuing a degree in a subject that fascinates you can provide intellectual stimulation, social engagement, and a sense of growth and accomplishment. Many universities offer special programs for older adults, and there are countless online learning resources available.

Relationships are also a crucial source of meaning and fulfillment in retirement. Nurturing connections with family and friends, spending quality time with loved ones, and forging new social bonds can provide a deep sense of belonging and support. Some retirees find joy in caring for grandchildren, reconnecting with old friends, or building community through shared interests and activities.

As you explore different avenues for purpose and fulfillment, remember that it's okay to experiment and change course. What brings you meaning at the start of retirement may shift over time as your circumstances and priorities evolve. The key is to remain open to new possibilities and to continue seeking out experiences that resonate with your deepest self.

Now, let's talk about leaving a legacy. A legacy is something that endures beyond your lifetime - a lasting impact on the people and world around you. It's the way you'll be remembered and the ongoing influence of your life's work and values.

For some, leaving a legacy means passing on financial resources to family members or charitable causes. This might involve estate planning to ensure your assets are distributed according to your wishes, or setting up a donor-advised fund or foundation to support the organizations and issues you care about most.

But a legacy is about more than just money. It's also about the stories, wisdom, and values you pass on to future generations. Consider writing an ethical will - a document that shares your life lessons, hopes, and beliefs with your loved ones. Or, record your personal history through a memoir, oral history, or video interviews.

Your legacy can also live on through the impact you've had on others. The lives you've touched, the careers you've mentored, the communities you've served - these are all part of the unique imprint you leave on the world. As you move through retirement, consider ways to continue making a positive difference, whether it's through formal roles or everyday acts of kindness and generosity.

Ultimately, finding purpose and leaving a legacy in retirement is about living a life that's true to yourself - a life that reflects your values, passions, and unique gifts. It's about using your time, talents, and resources to make the world a little brighter and to leave a positive mark that endures.

As you embark on this new chapter, remember that retirement is not an ending, but a beginning - a chance to explore new horizons, discover hidden depths, and create a life of meaning and fulfillment. By staying open to possibilities, seeking out experiences that resonate with your soul, and striving to make a difference in ways both big and small, you can craft a retirement that is truly rich in purpose and a legacy that will shine on long after you're gone.

www.ingramcontent.com/pod-product-compliance
Lightning Source LLC
Chambersburg PA
CBHW052206220526
45471CB00004B/1840